Cambridge
▶ **INTERA**

MW01179190

Series editor Bob Hastings

SAVED!
HEROES IN EVERYDAY LIFE

A1

Simon Beaver

CAMBRIDGE UNIVERSITY PRESS
Cambridge, New York, Melbourne, Madrid, Cape Town,
Singapore, São Paulo, Delhi, Mexico City

Cambridge University Press
32 Avenue of the Americas, New York, NY 10013-2473, USA

www.cambridge.org
Information on this title: www.cambridge.org/9781107647053

First published 2014
Reprinted 2014

Printed in Hong Kong, China, by Golden Cup Printing Company Limited

A catalog record for this publication is available from the British Library.

Library of Congress Cataloging-in-Publication Data

Beaver, Simon.
 Saved! : heroes in everyday life : level A1 / Simon Beaver.
    pages cm. -- (Cambridge discovery interactive readers)
  ISBN 978-1-107-64705-3 (pbk. : alk. paper)
1. Children--Biography--Juvenile literature. 2. Heroes--Biography--Juvenile literature.
3. Courage in children--Juvenile literature. 4. Readers (Elementary) 5. English language--
Textbooks for foreign speakers. I. Title.

CT107.B42 2014
920--dc23

                        2013014258

ISBN 978-1-107-64705-3

Additional resources for this publication at www.cambridge.org

Layout services, art direction, book design, and photo research: Q2ABillSMITH GROUP
Editorial services: Hyphen S.A.
Audio production: CityVox, New York
Video production: Q2ABillSMITH GROUP

Contents

Before You Read: Get Ready!

Heroes are people who do really great things. There are many different kinds of heroes.

Words to Know

Complete the sentences with the correct words.

climb   fight   save   accident

ground   costume   fire

1 In a house, we walk on the floor. Outside, we walk on the _____.

2 Spider-Man can _____ walls, and he wears a red and blue _____.

3 If you drive too fast, you can have an _____.

4 Cats and dogs are not usually friends. They often _____.

5 Look! There's a _____ in that house, and some people are there. We have to _____ them, or they will die!

Words to Know

Read the paragraph. Then complete the sentences with the correct highlighted words.

John of Gaunt was a son of King Edward III of England. He lived from 1340 to 1399. He was very tall: two meters! That's unusual. Not many people are two meters tall. John lived in a dangerous time. England was at war with France from 1369. John had to fight a lot, but he was a good fighter. He was good at riding horses, too. He never fell off his horse! John of Gaunt is a hero in England – a national hero.

John of Gaunt

❶ Rain _____ from the sky yesterday.

❷ An Olympic swimming pool is 50 _____ long from one end to the other.

❸ Don't walk in the street! That's very _____!

❹ Nelson Mandela is a _____ hero in South Africa.

❺ Today was an _____ summer day. It was very cold. I needed to wear a jacket.

❻ In the past, the most important person in a country was the _____.

❼ When countries use weapons to fight each other, they are _____.

5

CHAPTER 1

A Hero's Story: Tilly Smith

IN 2004, A TEN-YEAR-OLD ENGLISH GIRL CALLED TILLY SMITH LEARNED ABOUT TSUNAMIS IN HER CLASS AT SCHOOL.

Tilly's teacher, Andrew Kearney, told the children all about tsunamis. Tilly thought it was very interesting.

Only a week or two after that, Tilly went to Thailand with her mother, father, and sister. They stayed in Phuket, a favorite place for people on vacation. One day, Tilly and her family went to Maikhao Beach. Many people were there to enjoy the sun, go swimming, play games, and have a good time.[1]

[1] **have a good time:** enjoy something

A tsunami

Then Tilly saw something very unusual. The water began to leave the beach quickly! She remembered Mr. Kearney's lesson: it is dangerous when water leaves the beach fast. It shows that a tsunami is coming.

Tilly was worried. She told her mother and father about the water. They spoke to the other families on the beach and the people who worked in the hotels, too. They all left the beach. They quickly

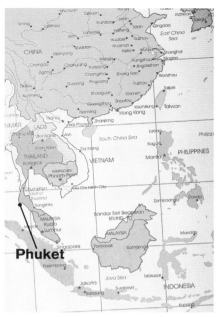

Phuket, Thailand

walked up to high ground, away from the water, and waited. And then the tsunami came. It was a wall of water. It was many meters tall!

People in other places had big problems, and many people died. But the people at Maikhao Beach were all safe. A ten-year-old girl **saved** them.

Tilly was a hero!

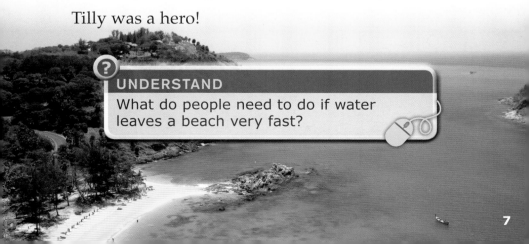

?

UNDERSTAND

What do people need to do if water leaves a beach very fast?

Spider-Man

CHAPTER 2

Superheroes

SUPER CAN MEAN "GREAT" OR "BETTER THAN NORMAL." SO SUPERHEROES CAN DO MORE THAN NORMAL PEOPLE – AND MORE THAN OTHER HEROES!

We all know Spider-Man and Superman with their famous costumes. Superman can do much more than us. He can fly, stop trains with his hands, **jump** over tall buildings,[2] and see through walls. These are his super powers.

In superhero stories, there are also villains. Villains do a lot of very bad things. The superhero's job is to stop the villain. Some villains are supervillains because they have super powers, too.

[2]**building:** schools and houses are kinds of buildings

In the Superman stories, Brainiac is a supervillain. He can fly like Superman, and he can move[3] things by thinking about them.

Many people like to read about superheroes or watch movies about them. It is fun for people to think about super powers. They think, "What super power would I like to have?"

Superheroes fight villains.

Of course, there aren't any superheroes in the world, and normal people do not have super powers. But who knows? Maybe one day…

[3]**move:** take something from one place and put it in another

Video Quest

Superhero

Watch the video about a new superhero. What can a gecko do?

CHAPTER 3

Folk Heroes

PEOPLE LOVE STORIES ABOUT HEROES. SOME OF THESE STORIES ARE VERY, VERY OLD.

Ishikawa Goemon

The Romans lived in Italy more than 2,000 years ago. They wrote about Spartacus. He was big and strong. He fought hard to help people. Today, Spartacus is a folk hero.

A folk hero is a hero that many people in a town or country know about. Usually, the story starts as a true story – a real[4] person does something dangerous or heroic.[5] People hear, remember, and tell the story year after year. The story changes and gets bigger and bigger. There are more and more stories. Soon, the real person is a folk hero, and the stories are folk stories.

[4]**real:** from the world, not from a book or a movie
[5]**heroic:** like a hero

Many folk heroes take money from rich[6] people and give it to poor people: Robin Hood in England, Ishikawa Goemon in Japan, Ustym Karmaliuk in Ukraine, and many others.

Many people say that folk heroes do not die; they are sleeping, and they wake up when their people need them. These folk heroes are often kings or famous people: Arthur in England, Charlemagne in Germany, El Cid in Spain, and others.

There are also many national heroes in different parts of the world. Simón Bolívar is a national hero in some countries in South America. He fought[7] the Spanish to help some South American people be **free**. People like to tell stories about him. In the future, he may be a folk hero!

[6]**rich:** having a lot of money
[7]**fought:** past of "fight"

Simón Bolívar

? APPLY
Think about some folk heroes or national heroes in your country. Who are they? What did they do?

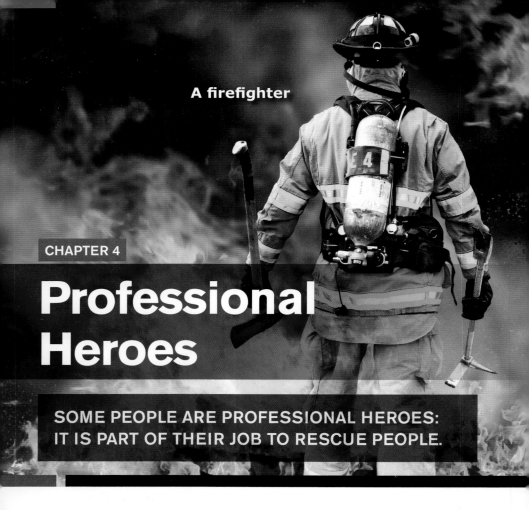

A firefighter

CHAPTER 4

Professional Heroes

SOME PEOPLE ARE PROFESSIONAL HEROES: IT IS PART OF THEIR JOB TO RESCUE PEOPLE.

The police stop people from doing bad things. Paramedics go to dangerous places to help people. Soldiers fight for their country in a war. Many people say that these people are heroes.

Think about firefighters. Is a firefighter a hero when he or she helps somebody leave a burning[8] house? It is dangerous work, but we pay firefighters to do this job – to fight **fire**. Are they really heroes?

[8]**burning:** on fire

Doctors save people.

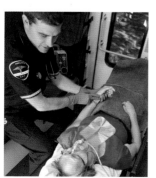

Paramedics save people, too.

Are doctors heroes when they save somebody's life? This is also difficult and important work, but we pay doctors to do it. And it is usually not dangerous for the doctors.

Paramedics have a much more dangerous job. They help people when there is an accident on the road. Sometimes they have to go into burning cars to **rescue** people. They also have to help **crazy** or dangerous people. Are paramedics more heroic than doctors?

Soldiers sometimes have to fight for their country. We usually call soldiers heroes if they save other soldiers when it's dangerous.

But soldiers don't always fight. Sometimes soldiers save people when there is a natural disaster, like a flood. In a flood, the water from rivers gets very high and goes into people's houses. Are soldiers heroes when they rescue people from natural disasters?

If a soldier is ready to fight or to save people, but there isn't a war and there isn't a natural disaster, is he or she still a hero?

A soldier after Hurricane Katrina

A police officer

Sometimes professionals do heroic things when they are not working. They can stop something bad or rescue somebody.

In Australia in 2011, police officer Raelene Longden was on a train after she left work. There was an accident. A man fell under the train. It was very dangerous, but Officer Longden jumped down and went under the train to help him. She saved his life.

Are police officers heroes only when they are not working? What about when they are working?

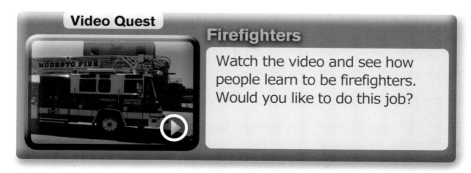

Video Quest

Firefighters

Watch the video and see how people learn to be firefighters. Would you like to do this job?

CHAPTER 5

Hero For a Day

SOMETIMES, PEOPLE DON'T WANT TO BE HEROES. THEY DON'T ASK TO BE HEROES. BUT DANGEROUS THINGS HAPPEN, AND THEY ARE HEROES.

In January 2009, a plane left New York City in the USA. There were a lot of big birds flying in the sky that day. After only three minutes in the **air**, the plane flew into some of the birds, and the plane stopped working. The pilot,[9] Captain Sullenberger, was really worried. "This is dangerous," he thought. "This plane cannot stay in the sky!"

He had to land[10] the plane quickly and safely. He looked down, but there was nowhere to go – only the Hudson River. He had to bring the plane down on the water – but not in the water.

....

[9] **pilot:** the person who flies the plane
[10] **land:** bring a plane from the sky to the ground

The plane in the Hudson River

People near the river watched the plane and waited. This was crazy! But he did it! The pilot landed the plane on the river!

All the passengers came out of the plane and stood on the plane's wings.[11] People came to the plane in boats and rescued the passengers. They were all safe. Everyone said that Captain Sullenberger was a hero.

Do you think Captain Sullenberger is a hero, or is he just a very good pilot? He helped many people that day, but he saved himself, too!

[11] **wing:** the long parts on both sides of a plane; birds also have two wings.

Captain
Sullenberger

Rescued passengers

In Brazil in 2007, a five-year-old boy called Riquelme Maciel was in his Spider-Man costume. He saw that there was a fire in a house. A baby girl was inside the house in her bed. Riquelme went into the house and took the baby outside. He rescued her from the fire.

Another "Spider-Man" saved a child in Thailand in 2009. A little boy climbed from a window in his school. He was very high above the ground, and he did not want to come down.

A firefighter heard his mother say that her son loved superheroes. He decided to wear a Spider-Man costume and went to the little boy. He told the boy that he wanted to save him. The little boy came to him.

Do you think the "Spider-Man" in both these stories is a hero?

Video Quest

Chilean Miners

Watch the video about some miners in Chile. How long did they have to stay in the mine?

Kids at a triathlon

CHAPTER 6

What Do You Think?

CONNER LONG HAS A YOUNGER BROTHER, CAYDEN. CAYDEN IS ALWAYS HAPPY, BUT HE'S VERY, VERY HAPPY WHEN THEY PLAY SPORTS TOGETHER.

Cayden Long is different from other children. He has a disability.[12] He cannot walk or talk much. His big brother, Conner, loves him and always helps him. Conner wanted to help Cayden play in a sports competition.[13] But how?

In 2011, Conner heard about the Children's Triathlon in Nashville, Tennessee, where they live. A triathlon is a competition where people run, ride bikes, and swim. He wanted to do the triathlon with Cayden. The triathlon people said, "OK!"

[12] **disability:** a problem that a person has with his or her body
[13] **competition:** something people try to win by being the best, fastest, etc

In the swimming part, Conner took Cayden in a small boat. In the running and bike-riding parts of the competition, Cayden rode in a chair on wheels, like a small car. The two brothers finished all three parts of the competition together. They were not first, but they were not last!

"If I work hard and I say 'I can,' then I can," said Conner.

So who is the hero? Is it Conner, who does so much to make his little brother happy? Is it Cayden, who has a disability but really enjoys life? Or are they both heroes?

Nashville, TN

After You Read

Read the sentences and choose Ⓐ (True) or Ⓑ (False). If the book does not tell you, choose Ⓒ (Doesn't say).

1 Phuket is in Japan.

- Ⓐ True
- Ⓑ False
- Ⓒ Doesn't say

2 Superman can swim the Atlantic Ocean.

- Ⓐ True
- Ⓑ False
- Ⓒ Doesn't say

3 Simón Bolívar is a national hero in more than one country.

- Ⓐ True
- Ⓑ False
- Ⓒ Doesn't say

4 Soldiers sometimes help people if there is a flood.

- Ⓐ True
- Ⓑ False
- Ⓒ Doesn't say

5 The police officer Raelene Longden fell under a train.

- Ⓐ True
- Ⓑ False
- Ⓒ Doesn't say

6 Captain Sullenberger has a wife and children.

- Ⓐ True
- Ⓑ False
- Ⓒ Doesn't say

7 In a triathlon, people run, ride bikes, and swim.

- Ⓐ True
- Ⓑ False
- Ⓒ Doesn't say

Complete the Chart

Write the names of your three favorite heroes. What did / do they do? Why are they your favorite heroes?

Name	What they did / do	Why you like them

Complete the Text

Write one word in each space.

Captain Sullenberger was a very good ❶ _____.
His plane flew into some ❷ _____. He flew the plane
down to a ❸ _____ called the Hudson. People used
❹ _____ to get the passengers from the plane.

Answer Key

Words to Know, page 4
1 ground **2** climb, costume **3** accident **4** fight
5 fire, save

Words to Know, page 5
1 fell **2** meters **3** dangerous **4** national **5** unusual
6 king **7** at war

Understand, page 7
They need to leave the beach, quickly walk up to high ground away from the water, and wait.

Video Quest, page 9
A gecko can climb walls.

Apply, page 11
Answers will vary.

Video Quest, page 15
Answers will vary.

Video Quest, page 19
69 days

True or False, page 22
1 B **2** C **3** A **4** A **5** B **6** C **7** A

Complete the Chart, page 23
Answers will vary.

Complete the Text, page 23
1 pilot **2** birds **3** river **4** boats